EVENTS MANAGEMENT

COLOR OF EVENTS

SANJEEV SRIVASTAVA

DEDICATION

My Mothers –

[LATE] Mrs. Vibha Srivastava
Mrs. Mithilesh Singh

It is because of Almighty whose Blessings got this Book completed and Published. And then My Mothers Girths were my Inspirations all the way along.

CONTENTS

EVENTS MANAGEMENT

COLOR OF EVENTS

By -

Sanjeev Srivastava

CHAPTER 1

ORIGIN OF EVENTS

Man is a social animal. He used to live in caves during ancient times. His main activities were hunting and sex. As time passed, man came out of such caves and wandered long distances to know more about his surroundings. Slowly he left caves and made cave like huts in plains. He cleared jungles and his huts were made of mud and tree branches. Their developed colony of huts and specialized groups became prominent. These groups hunted or made huts.

Slowly these kinds of colonies took to enjoying their hunting or making huts. It became like a game and this were the basis of events. During such time whole group used to enjoy such kind of events. They used to run and make the animal fear out of their shouts and howling. Then they killed their prey. Hunting was thus a major source of enjoyment and this event was common in all groups of ancient civilization.

As time passed, man witnessed many natural phenomena like lightening and rain, day and night, summer and winter. Such kind of changes man could not understand and so they thought about God and Devil. He started worshipping such kind of Gods like Sun God, Moon God, Fire God, Devil God and Spirits. Later worshipping became another major event in the life of ancient man.

Civilizations developed and man created differentiations in his society. Business became prominence in all groups of ancient history. Slowly kingdoms came in limelight and King ruled such kingdoms.

The orders of king were the law of such kingdoms. Peoples had lots of free time and they formed 'Army' to fight other rulers.

By medieval time many kingdoms flourished and their army specialized in fighting. Sword and archery were developed and it became a new kind of game. Wrestling was also developed. Big lands were converted into 'Stadium grounds' and yearly games were conducted in these stadiums which whole mass of peoples and king and ministers of the kingdoms used to see. These yearly games were thus patronized by king and winners of these games used to get prizes. These games were so famous that it was conducted in all kingdoms round the globe.

Lots of new sports were discovered and rules were

made. Slowly such events created a sense of craze in the masses and they started playing these games in small grounds and in their homes. They practiced such games and prepared themselves for yearly games. Many games like bull fighting and lion fighting have a historical trace. Cricket, hockey and many more games have a recent origin and these games have become famous in modern era. Olympic game and ASIAD Games are certain world events, which has shrouded whole world in the spirit of brotherhood.   Cricket   is another game, which is famous event round the globe. Such events have the patrons of nations round the world.

In today's world, there are many corporate giants like Pepsi, Coca Cola and Sahara India which conduct cricket as a major sport event in many nations around the globe.

Similarly there are many other organizations that conduct other sport events like football, hockey, baseball, basketball, and volleyball; round the globe. In such events usually best players get lots of prizes and money.

Thus, we can conclude that Events Management is the conduction of any one or more events in the same participation with proper rules and public management in such a manner that the message of brotherhood and corporate or nations which are conducting the event – their publicity and messages reaches the masses around the globe in proper sense.

We thus witness cricket matches very well organized with no problems on part of the public and the match conducting organization and nation delivering their messages such that it reaches the masses around the globe in its proper sense. This is only an example of events management and lots of more such events are witnessed throughout the world daily.

Media is playing a lion's share in popularizing all such events. In newspapers, magazines and television sets we can visualize

such   events   daily   in
abundance.

CHAPTER 2

<u>TYPES OF EVENTS</u>

When we hear about events we are filled with a sense of joy and we wait eagerly for the conduction date of such events. There is a sense of pomp and show and we prepare ourselves for such events like clothing, tickets or passes and organizing our friend circle to go for the event. If an event is conducted by an organization or a nation then the peoples of such places are filled with a sense of pride first because it is their nation or organization that is conducting such event. Even nation or organizations spend lots of money in the conduction of such events. For such event conducting places, their sense of pride far envelopes the sense of victory and they mainly spread a message of goodness and brotherhood in the glorious events through the participants.

Today events have traced a long history ever since ancient times and it is the best means of enjoyment and recreation. Peoples not only enjoy such events but also are fans of such events and their participants. Any event or participant of events arouse such a kind of enthusiasm in the Psychos of the masses that they become totally engrossed in it and forget all their worries and tension. For them, their participants are idols and they must not only do well in the events but also must win.

Thus events are branded around the globe as per the taste of people such that events are of different variety. Various events are described as under –

1. **<u>Minor Events</u>** - These are small events occurring in day to day activities of peoples' life at which peoples give practically no thoughts. Such events can range from day robbery, small gathering of peoples for their demands, office lunch break and employees sharing and praising each others' Tiffin, accident news in newspapers and so on. Such minor events are like lubricants in peoples'

life which keeps them recreationally busy though practically such events have no prominent significance in the lives of peoples.

2. **<u>Parties and Conferences</u>** - Such events are of major significance for the participants of the event and also for the masses at large. Women enjoy kitty parties and learn a lot from it about their surroundings and families that makes

them socially aware and enthusiastic about their nation. Organizations conduct parties and staffs learn new things from the speech and gathering.

Conferences and symposiums are conducted by colleges, universities, research organizations and councils where intellectuals share their views and these views and new researches coming in news are of great implications to the masses throughout the world.

3. **<u>Cultural programs and Festivals</u>** - Every nation or organization or society has a history through which it has developed to present eminence and even present would be a history in future era when there would be more development in the nations. Thus what is today present would be a history

tomorrow and the base of this future era would be the past history and present which would also be a history. Thus every personality or idol and events leaves behind it a remembrance that is reminiscent year after year. Under such category we witness events like Independence Day, Christmas, New Year Day, Valentine Day, Teachers Day, Children Day and

Deepawali. Such events are cultural programs and festivals of various nations and they are celebrated around the globe enthusiastically with pomp and show and a message of Universal brotherhood and peace. It is well noted that Pope at Vatican gives a message of peace on 'Christmas Day', which were the message of God Jesus Christ.

4. **<u>Functions</u>** - Events occur in the life of peoples also like birthday parties or marriage functions which the families organize in order to solemnize and celebrate birthday or marriage of their family members. Even death of a deceased leads to cremation ceremony and a function. Thus our whole life is associated with such functions and according to the functions a similar

gathering response is seen which may be that of laughter or gloom.

5. **<u>Commercials and Stage Shows</u>** - Various organizations or individuals wish to popularize their products through models. These products can be anything from a sewing needle to a spacecraft. Usually, these events are seen in corporate sector or in media where the

products or views of the organization or individual are lime-lighted and taken to the masses to develop a kind of image for such products or views in their minds. The better such commercial film or stage show is conducted with models of imminence; the better would be the response from the public regarding such products or views. It is thus on the response of the public through such a publicity propaganda that the products or views are sold in the market. The publicity thus is the sole responsibility of media to popularize such events.

6. **<u>Rallies and Strikes</u>** - Usually in nations, society gets perturbed by the malpractices and misadministration on part of government authorities. They resort to mob

gathering and violent activities clashing with police and authorities and destroying anything in vicinity. They are in a shameful trance of destruction and obey no words till their demands, which are mostly genuine, are fulfilled. Such kind of events also happen as a curse in society and no society around the globe is free from such an event. It is the fault of both government and peoples for the occurrence of such events in society because it is the peoples who choose wrong government and when government does not work which is the fault of the government, then peoples go for rallies and strikes leading to curfew and chaos in the nations.

7. **<u>Big Sports Sponsoring Events</u>** - There are association of nations in

our world which organize various sports events like Olympic Games and ASIAD Games at Four Years interval. Also, in many nations there are health marathon race and marathon walks. Various big corporate giants conduct big sports event like cricket matches and car race. There is special television channels dedicated to media for popularizing all sorts of sports events throughout the world. Even newspapers have special sports page and there are sports magazines related with various sports.

Governments throughout the world spend fortune on popularizing various sports events. Football is a European tournament, which is very popular among nations. These sports event are sponsored by big corporate giants and have the patrons of various nations that are conducting it.

Events can also be categorized as small event, medium event and large-scale event depending upon the money, time and masses witnessing such events. Cricket and football matches, Olympic and ASIAD Sports event are large-scale events throughout the nations.

Political rally of significance are medium events while small events can be like a robbery in the neighbourhood.

Thus we have witnessed various kinds of events in our day-to-day activities. These events lubricate us and we have a topic to discuss in our home, neighborhood or friend circle. We enthusiastically many times have participated in various events also. Today, events are a profession which many personalities practices round the globe. Name the field and event participants would be found in it.

CHAPTER 3

DECIDING AN EVENT

Individuals, families, organizations or nations organize events. Usually, before organizing any event, it is essential to analyze all aspects of such events. It is first discussed what kind of event is to be organized. Depending upon the kind of ceremony, the organizers decide the event and give it the shape of inception – that is, they set the beginning of the event. They decide an avenue where the event would be held. Depending upon the events shape, the avenue should be accordingly decided.

We have to decide the budget of the event. Whoever the organizers are they have to check on their purse before conducting the event. They have to thus budget the event. All aspects of the event are taken into consideration and accordingly money has to be allotted to each aspect of the event so that the events are properly managed and funded. Money plays very important role in the life of peoples. Because of such events, people earn a livelihood for themselves.

Thereafter list of invitees is made by which peoples who are invited would come to events. Even tickets and passes for certain events are arranged. Usually these tickets and passes are valued for such events, and people visiting such events have thus to pay money. They enjoy the event and make full use of their money and presence. The peoples visiting such events thus enjoy events as bonanza of happiness and recreation.

Events have to be publicized also so that the number of peoples visiting the events is in plenty. Certain events are only publicized with the message and such events do not want masses to come. Thus depending upon the type of events, publicity is accordingly done. Media plays an important role in publicizing the events.

The events are witnessed by masses around the world. Thanks to the media coverage who are present round the clock picturing and reporting the event on television and in newspapers and magazines. The whole event may also be video covered through modern technologies video cameras and also compact discs (CDs) are made of important events. Thus media makes the masses round the globe aware about the events and its schedule. The messages of the events are well highlighted by media.

Today deciding and conducting an event requires security arrangements as well for professionals who are worshipped as 'Idols Participants' in such events. Thus police and intelligence agencies play a major role in the security of the events arrangement.

Schedule of the events are also publicized so that peoples come to know about the programs of the events. Peoples accordingly prepare themselves for the events program according to the schedule of the events.

CHAPTER 4

SURVEYS AND RESULT OF EVENTS

What event is to be organized depends upon the ceremony in families and accordingly a birthday party or marriage function is organized. For such functions there is no need of conducting a survey because such an event is the ceremony of the family.

However, big nations or

organizations conduct big sports matches and thus survey becomes necessary for deciding the various aspects of events including the type of events. For such survey work there are big companies, which through Public Relation Professionals (PROs), conduct the survey work. The PROs carry a pamphlet of questionnaires and visit houses and shopkeepers and peoples on the street.

They meet them and ask the questions of the questionnaire, which are related to the events basically, and fill the questionnaire. Thus from the masses, the PROs form a general survey report about the conduction of the event. It is thus seen that while Cricket match is famous in Asia, Football match is famous in Europe. Also, the types of clothes and colour of the clothes and the culture of the masses are certain questions that the PROs ask in order to affirm the various aspects of the event. Thus events are decided and all the aspects of the events are discussed after consulting the survey questionnaire and a general outlook for conducting the event is chalked out which may as well be statistically.

While the event is running, the PROs, Interviewers and Reporters are all on their feet and question the public and participants, and accordingly result their views in a general sense. Though the minority views are also considered but the views of the majority hold a greater importance. These views are graphed statistically and a survey event report is formulated. These reports are then matched throughout the world and in a global sense we come to know of the event report. Thus it is found that while Baseball is liked in America and is the national game of USA; Hockey is liked in India and is the national game of India.

Depending on the result of the event survey reports, we can come to know of the culture, tastes and attitudes of peoples throughout the world. These events thus play an important role in quilting the nations of the world. A sports loving nation would also like to be brotherly in attitudes. Peoples would be recreational and happy. A nation where strikes and rallies are common, there peoples would be of destructive mentality and negative in attitudes and more dishonest.

Thus we see that the events are a matter for intellectuals

through its survey and end result reports, as per which the various aspects of the events are highlighted. These reports give the taste of the peoples for various events throughout the world and such surveys are global phenomenon.

CHAPTER 5

<u>NATIONAL EVENTS AND ITS IMPORTANCE</u>

Each nation round the globe is a bundle of personalities and events. Days like Independence Day and Birthday of Father of Nation are very important event for the Nation. Similarly, holidays are given on certain holy festivals like Deepawali and Christmas Day which are the festival of crackers and birthday of God Jesus Christ respectively. Such kind of National events are a matter of rejoicing for the whole nation. Peoples celebrate such events with great pomp and show.

These National events have great implication on the lives of the citizens. Apart from taking such events as a major means of recreation and rejoicing, peoples are embossed in the same cultural phenomenon celebrating the event in a national sequence. Thus if Deepawali is celebrated in India then in all parts of India; houses would be decorated with candle light and crackers would be busted. This is common in whole of India and this is the culture of Deepawali festival in India.

Such event lubricates the lives of the peoples throughout Nation and it gives a sense of enthusiasm among the peoples. They wait eagerly for such events to come and celebrate it. They discuss the various aspects of events and cultivate a sense of event craze among themselves. They thus on Christmas Day, for example, in America discuss the birth of God Jesus Christ in Jerusalem and are engrossed in singing Christmas carols before the event. In full pomp and show, Christmas festival grips the Nation in Christmas fervour almost a month before the festival. Many programs come on television sets in America. Peoples thus talk Christmas and enjoy the whole festival month in America.

On the main event day or the schedules of the event, peoples throng in masses at the avenues where the event is held. For example if cricket match is held then peoples in mass visit the stadium to witness the match and they enjoy it thoroughly. Peoples in cars, buses, taxis and walking come to Stadium. Those who are not keen in coming to stadium sit at home and through the excellent media coverage, enjoy the match at home. It's a 'MATCH MASS' in stadium and in the whole nation which witness the match.

The peoples round the Nation on events day are enthralled in a sense of brotherhood enjoying the event in the same manner as brothers enjoy at home. Thus whole nation can be seen as a brotherly home of the masses. They discuss the same event, wear alike clothes and eat alike food during the same event, enjoy the same event in the same sense of recreation and send out to the world the same message from their nation. They thus give the sense of 'NATIONAL PRIDE' and whole nation is in the same national brotherhood. Thus events are of great importance in bringing the peoples together on such events day.

CHAPTER 6

INTERNATIONAL EVENTS AND ITS IMPORTANCE

There are certain events which have international implications. Such events to name a few of them are 'Valentine Day', 'May Day', 'Labour Day' and 'Teachers Day'. Such events are chalked out by United Nation Organization and are universally recognized. Whole of world nations accept such events in its national agenda of events.

These events are like the gifts of society of world and great world leaders and so such events have world implications. Peoples throughout the world recognize such events in remembrance of such world societies and world leaders. Whole world is gripped in the same   sense   of   event recreation.

On such days of events, peoples in masses listen to their nation and other nation leaders' speech and spread the message of brotherhood and Universal peace to whole world. Such messages can be read in all leading dailies and magazines and also witnessed on television sets. Thus whole world becomes a culture and event as the means of tying the whole world in the same brotherly thread. Peoples enthusiastically arrange programs round the world and it is a matter of great intra-cultural brotherhood and inter-cultural brotherhood which can be seen.

Nobody is left out on such days. Even organizations and families arrange small cultural programs on such days to enjoy the events ethics among themselves. Thus these world events lubricate nations with the oil of brotherhood and even enemy nations on such days become friends.

On Valentine Day for example, peoples round the globe send the Valentine Cards to their friends and whole world rejoice this Universal brotherly thread events. Not only boys and girls but children and elders are also a part of Valentine Day events participations. Thus whole world witnesses a thread festival on Valentine Day. Great leaders deliver speech on this day and cultural programs are held in big clubs and hotels where peoples tie valentines thread knot on the wrist of each other becoming great friends like brothers are. Thus Valentine's Day is a recreational event round the globe.

On such international events, usually offices remain closed so that peoples enjoy the events in its proper sense at home and in their Society of Friends circle. It is a great cultural transition from one nation to another and peoples learn a lot on such events day from other nation peoples. They accordingly change their lives for their betterment and their attitudes exhibit a variety of feelings pertaining to whole world. It is a real blend of world society on such events. Today world really needs such events in order to shed enmity among the nations and live in the true spirit of brotherhood.

CHAPTER 7

EVENTS POLITICIZATION AND WORLD POLITY

Modern World is the horserace of Superpower-ism and Egoistic Superiority over others. Whole world is divided into developed nations and developing nations. Developed nations are those where the whole nation is fully developed and proper law and order is maintained in the nation because of which peoples are industrious and have made their nation rich like USA, UK, France and Russia. Developing nations are those where development process is not yet complete and proper law and order is not followed in the nation and peoples are frustrated such that such nations have less national income capita. Thus such nations are mediocre nations monetarily and are in the poverty line of the world. Such nations gets fund from developed nations or World Bank or World Monetary Fund and thus survive for their existence. Rich nations are so developed that they are superpowers and feed many nations round the globe through their aids and funds. Thus developing nations are poor nations and apart from national income, they need funds from World and other developed nations.

Based on the above criterion of nation demarcation on development, it is seen that events are also politicized. Superpowers and Developed Nations seldom participate together in the same event because such events can become the battlefield ground and a cause of great wars. Thus USA and Russia have been boycotting Olympic Games alternately. In one Olympiad USA participate while in the next Olympiad Russia participates. To avoid such wars, events round the globe have been politicized and major confronts have been avoided. Thus though the real sense of brotherhood in world is to be given through such events, but politicization of such events is necessary otherwise there would be World battles.

Many nations wish to express their superiority over other

nations because of such events and such superiority expression mars the true spirit of event organizers. For example on Christmas Day, while it is a World event, certain developed nation's Church Fathers' impose on the world their nation's superiority instead of spreading the Christmas Day message of God Jesus Christ Birthday.

There are certain political events which we have been witnessing like nuclear treaty and world trade treaty. Such treaties only express the dictatorial attitudes of developed superpowers to conquer world and make other nations their slaves. Many nations today have openly expressed their revolt against such treaties and thus such political treaties events have lost its true meaning and have been shrouded the sheet of extinction.

One very good example of politicizing events can be witnessed in India – Pakistan Cricket Series. During the cricket match between India – Pakistan, cricket mongers from various nations witness the real battle and aggressive attitudes of the peoples of the two nations. It is said that India – Pakistan Cricket matches are as if war between India and Pakistan, which mongers witness.

It is really a matter of immense displeasure when we witness events getting politicized round the globe. It should be noted that events are not battlefields for nations. World must learn to enjoy the event differently in the spirit of brotherhood and a sense of disciplined peace. War or politicizing of events does not mean that events would end. Events must be learnt to be recreational and not fight over it like spoilt children. It is a matter of pride for the organizers of the events and such events thus should not be politicized otherwise the organizers would tearfully adieu the event.

World Society has still to become one and whenever

those events which bring together the nations of the world are held; such events should be truly enjoyed in the proper sense. It is not world polity which gives such events the shape of brotherhood but it is the masses throughout the world who are the real brotherhood beneficiary of such events. Thus peoples should keep politics away from events and participate happily in the events with the true spirit of events and enjoy the event thoroughly.

CHAPTER 8

CRIMINALIZATION OF EVENTS

In events, important dignitaries and professionals who have a number of fans round the globe; participate. Thus these events are very important and criminals make most of such events. In history, there has been news of bombarding event avenues and many deaths of viewers and participants have been reported. Such criminalization of events has tarnished the sportsman spirit of events.

It has been found that international professional criminals have bribed players or event organizers in order to favor the events result in their interests. There is lots of broker-aegis involved in such events. Peoples put huge amount of money as brokerage promise regarding events and the winners walk away with the huge share of money. Such kind of gambling have invited the interests of international criminals and resulted in pantheism of events.

There has been news of conspiracies against many famous edentates. Certain event idols have been given life threats by these criminals. Criminals get lots of money from peoples and nations to kidnap and kill edentates. Criminals need money and they do not bother about the reputation of the event idols. It is really a heinous crime. One of the famous killing conspiracies has been the death of famous Martial Arts Expert Bruce Lee. Moreover, news of this kind has been that of Charlie Chaplin the famous yesteryears comedian whose dead body was dug and a huge amount of ransom money was demanded.

In Cricket and football matches, trillions of Dollars are changing hands today as brokers involve themselves. In

Europe and England trillions of Dollars are put on bet and it is a common scenario there. There have been cases of horse trading as well in which peoples buy event idols and ask them to perform as per their wish. Lots of nations have lost trophies and team spirits because of such horse trading.

Even political leaders and their government agencies are involved in illegitimating events. One of the important examples has been that of American President John F. Kennedy's brother who used to get kidnap famous American Actress Marilyn Monroe and rape her. This had become a daily event and finally when Actress asked to marry; he refused as a result of which Actress committed suicide. Such kind of heinous crime from such important personalities has been witnessed. President Bill

Clinton and Monica Lewinsky sex scandal has been another shameful event in World History. Pamela Bordes an Indian bred call girl of high society has been highly active in Britain. Mohammed Ali the famous boxer of World level had become victim of AIDS – an incurable disease of present era because of having multiple sexes which were arranged.

Today events criminalization has become deep rooted and adequate security measures are taken. Security loopholes are studied and prevented. In near future tight security arrangements have been planned.

CHAPTER 9

<u>HI – TECH EVENTS</u>

Today Events are a matter of household talks. Events are involved in the lives of peoples as if they are themselves participants. Peoples discuss all aspects of events with great enthusiasm. In this era of events, high technology is playing a very significant role. Computers have come as a major event technology thereafter which space technology DTH have redefined events as Hi-Tech. Media cameras, videos and electronic technology now gear the rear place.

Computer technology have come up with computer games and video games which are installed in shops and peoples of all age group and especially children crowd such shops to play. In such games there are car race driving, crossing the river games; and it is real fun playing such games. Computer corporation giants like Microsoft are inventing new games and such games after certifications are coming in markets in large scale. In many nations where peoples are rich, they buy such games and keep it in their home for their personal use.

Space technology plays an important role in events. An

event which is being held in India can be visualized in USA thousands of kilometres far away because of space technology. Many nations today have their own satellites. These satellites are having transponders. Thus when an event is held in India; signals go from transmitting cameras to satellites in space and get reflected by its transponders round the globe which are received by antennas of television sets and thus such events are visualized round the globe. Viewers witness in their home on their television sets the minute details of events with the masses in such avenues; and receive the message generated.

Electronics have made a great revolution in Camera Technology and various kinds of cameras are in market and with reporters of dailies who are present in the avenues of events, capturing all minute details of the events on the reels of cameras. The sports reporters accordingly make various types of video U-matic and general video tapes which are sold to various television channels and peoples. These video tapes have a similar kind of CDs (compact discs) and these tapes and CDs are played on Video and CD sets and peoples thus witness such events on their television sets. It is the era of digital cameras and digital technology and thus the events can be witnessed in a much better sense as if the viewers are themselves in the fields or in avenues witnessing such events. The clarity of picture and sound has really become great because of electronic revolution in the field of digital cameras.

Even print media has witnessed a great revolution. Newspapers and magazines picture and word prints including the page layout are such that its' just fabulous reading and visualizing news through print media.

Robots and holography are certain advanced hi-tech technologies of future era and three dimensional picturing of events are also a matter of significance.

CHAPTER 10

I

SPONSORING OF EVENTS

Events are a global phenomenon which involves expenditure accordingly. Family arrange their events out of their savings and its' their money worth.

There are large scale events where huge expenditures are

involved and it is thus only in the capacity of excessively rich businessmen of world or organizations or nations or a group of nations who patron and sponsor such events. It is such kind of big and rich organizers who budget all aspects of events so that events are not lacking in funds. Money plays very important role in funding events. Without big money, events are not organized. Events thus through proper sponsoring and patronizing becomes a matter of great pomp and show and it is as if the whole organizing staffs are transformed in a manner of great discipline and hosts.

The peoples of such organizing nations or organizations are engulfed in a sense of pride and they send out the message of events and universal peace and sportsman spirit round the globe. The whole world witnesses this spirit and also visualizes their participant idols in such events performing and putting in their best.

Certain sponsors of Cricket match are huge three corporate giants like Pepsi of USA, Coca-Cola of U.K. and Sahara India of India. It is a sense of pride and gratification in these sponsors while organizing such events and their message of sportsman spirit lubricates the lives of masses round the globe.

Today events sponsoring is a global phenomenon. Car race, Marathon walks and races and football are certain more events apart from cricket matches which are sponsored by huge corporate giants and nations. Even wrestling is another world sponsored event.

In media arena various films and commercials including Oscar awards are also sponsored and funded by producers and producer associations. Beauty contests are also organized leading to selection of Miss World and Miss Universe and these contests are also budgeted by nations and big media groups.

Political events are also sponsored by political parties

and big leaders. They receive funds from donations also. Thus such events are also well budgeted by its patrons.

Today we thus witness a number of events and in the past, many events have been held which has become history. In future also many events would be held. All such events require lots of money and sponsors would provide funds for such events so that the events are conducted in full pomp and show and peoples enjoy it thoroughly. Even the participants of such events gets well deserved prizes from sponsors and sponsors spread their message of sportsmanship, peace and brotherhood to World.

CHAPTER 11

II

SPONSORING OF EVENTS

Events are a matter of pride for the peoples of the organizations and nations organizing such events. Participants round the globe perform in such events and put in their best with the aim to win. In such events, we witness a number of haphazard dangerous to participants and viewers present in the venue. Peoples round the globe are witnessing these events. Keeping in view all this, security arrangements are essential so that no casualties happen in event avenues.

Political rallies and strikes where violent moles are witnessed require good security so that minimum casualties happen. Tear gas, lathi charge and putting whole area under curfew are the only security means for such mobs.

Events may be politicked or criminalized or abused which jeopardize the whole event thus essential to provide high profile security arrangements.

Participants who are worshipped round the globe as idols have greater risk to their life as well as their kidnapping and demand for ransom money. In past, event avenues have become a place of weapon fight and many peoples' including participants have lost their lives.

Nations have trained their security personals for all kinds of events. They have trained them into commando warfare and during events such security personnel are placed at all important city routes and outside the avenues of events thus avoiding any conflicts around avenues of such events or in city.

Proper security personals from police and intelligence agencies are placed at the gates of the event avenues and plain clothes man from police are present throughout the avenues of the events in order to check the nuisances created by the viewers. Policemen are scattered outside the avenues and all routes of the event avenues are minutely scrutinized.

Whole of the event avenue is put on media hi-tech scrutiny. Hi-tech miniature cameras are installed and a control room is set where the entire avenue is watched by police officers on television monitors. Wireless messages are sent from the control-room to policemen in the avenue to manage the security properly.

Even the air and atmosphere of the event avenue is watched to monitor humidity, rain and foul smell in the avenue. Even poisonous gas which may happen through criminalization of events is checked by installing gas soaking equipments in the avenue of the events. If rain happens then avenues are covered so that rain does not spoil the avenues.

Thus today security measures are very important in events. Peoples do not pelt participants with tin cans are also checked. Security measures are studied for various events. However because of politics, there are lapses in security measures of events and deaths of Smt. Indira Gandhi and Shri Rajiv Gandhi are important security lapses because of events politicization.

CHAPTER 12

BENEFICIARIES OF EVENTS

The organizers of events are the real beneficiaries' of events for it gives reputation and name to the organizers for conducting such magnificent event. Their messages reach far and wide which adds to the reputation and goodwill of the organizers. The income generated by the event goes in the purse of the organizers.

The stalls and seating arrangements including the stadium and avenue cost have to be borne by the organizers. The vendors' who supply such arrangements thus earn a major share of the events income. Also lighting arrangement vendor and media peoples who provide coverage of the events gets money and special allowances.

Vendor stalls like cold drinks and small eats vendor shops

selling pop corns and ice creams including lunch and snacks earn a good amount from these events. Peoples buy whatever they wish to from these vendor shops.

Security personals are also paid special allowances while the events are on. They get free tickets and passes for their family members. At many event places, security personnel are provided free food and lodging.

Even comics, Magazines and newspaper stalls are set up in the vicinity of events avenues. Peoples purchase their choice reading materials thus giving money to these magazine vendors.

At such avenues small toilets and bathrooms are set up where peoples relive themselves for small token of money. These toilet vendors earn money thus.

The incomes from such events are also diverted to prominent professionals of yesteryears who have grown old and are unable to manage their livelihood. Such professional gets money, which though is less, yet, sufficient for them for the time being to manage their important works.

The participants of the events get huge applause and praise from public and they get money and gifts from the organizers of the events which is the main livelihood source of such participants. Even big corporate giants and Governments give titles and jobs to such event-stars of brilliance. They are given free professional training in order to make their performances better in events.

The Nations who organize such events get good name on the map of International events because of which the sense of brotherhood spreads round the globe. Such Nations for their development and well being get easily their funds and aids from other nations which are developed and rich.

Charity funds are also given by event organizers. Many charitable trusts and organization earn money from such events thus providing free services to peoples at large.

Thus we have seen above mentioned beneficiaries of events. Peoples witnessing such events get real action treat for themselves from such events. Events must be conducted round the globe because many people earn their livelihood from such events.

CHAPTER 13

COMMERCIALIZATION OF EVENTS

Conducting an event requires huge amount of money. Such kind of money has to be arranged by organizers. They get money from big corporate giants or Government treasuries after approving their events. Thus corporations and Government sponsor and are patrons of these event organizers. For example for conducting cricket matches, it is impossible for World Cricket Board to organize matches unless it has money and various Nations' Patron-hood. Only then such matches can be conducted on large scale.

Even small organizations give their sponsorship to such events. They give money to such events so that adequate fund is possible. Banners and Posters are also placed in avenues of the events as patron-hood and sponsorship money for such events.

Tickets and fares are taken from public. They buy tickets for money so that events get funds. Thus peoples also give money for events to be held.

A part of National income is utilized in conduction of such events of importance. Today, not only nation but whole world is involved in giving money as part of their income tax or any other tax to their Government for conducting events with great pomp and show.

Today, even individuals and fans give big donations for conducting events. Thus fashion houses sponsor and organize fashion shows for which they give big amount of money as donation and charity. Stage shows are organized because of such donations.

Thus in modern world, events are getting commercialized and even small events are organized in lots of vagabond and extravaganza. Rat race for commercialization of events is on and can be witnessed in today's world. Society likes the pomp and crowd turning up in the event.

One question surely arises in

the minds of peoples after witnessing the amount of money going waste on such events. They realize that their money is going waste and proper utility of their money has not taken place. The organizers were more bent in spreading their whims than spending money in proper conduction of events. The real spirits of events thus takes a back place in the era of commercialization of events.

Today lots of events are getting conducted on large scale and huge amount of money is spent for commercializing such events. It is alright if such commercialization is properly done and money is properly utilized. Even events participants sometimes give poor performances thus frustrating their viewers and not giving them their money worth. Thus event-stars should give their best performances or give others a chance to perform so that public gets its money worth.

Commercialization of events must be avoided and true spirit of events must be enchanted.

CHAPTER 14

ARE EVENTS NECESSITY OR NATIONAL LOSS

Events lubricate the lives of peoples. Peoples and children from all walks of life discuss enthusiastically the various aspects of events. They are so much obsessed by events and its performers that they neglect other important activities of life. They take leave from their schools and offices in order to attend events. Thus it can be seen that events craze the lives of people to such an extent that during event schedules; it is just event for peoples and nothing else.

Events also are a mean of livelihood for many. Vendors and event-stars earn money from such events. Their main survivals are these events and money reaches their pockets. Even criminal and politicians gain money, image and reputation because of such events.

However, it is seen that events are held for months together. Lots of time is spent during these events. Money and time of Nation is spent in proper conduction of such events for months. National Money and National Time loss is thus witnessed while Nation only gains popularity and funds. Offices are vacant, employees stick to television and radio sets witnessing the events details. They neglect their office work. Also they stick to reading newspapers and magazines of such events and completely neglect daily routine of offices.

Because of this office neglect by employees, big long events like cricket test matches are getting curbed and today such matches are limited to one day match and a total of five or six matches of such kind are held. Thus previously these matches used to be held for months together while in today's time such matches finish within a fortnight thus limiting the National loss.

It is a fact that events though are necessary for peoples yet such events are a National loss because of the work neglect of peoples in order to attend the events. Peoples must be properly made aware about various types of events and must learn the recreations of events. They must not neglect their office works. If they have free time only then must they satisfy their enthusiasm about such events. Today work is very essential for peoples in competitive world. Even children must know that their Home-works are essential for shaping their future and not events. Only when they are free from their school work must they enjoy events.

Schools come first and also Offices comes first in children and peoples' lives respectively. Then comes' Events.

In many Developed Nations, events which spoil National Time and National Money; such events are given a secondary treatment. Cricket Matches are seldom seen in America while a day's baseball match is enthusiastically viewed by Americans.

CHAPTER 15

EVENTS ABUSE

In modern era, a phase has developed in which events are abused. By abuse of events it is meant that events were improperly conducted. Any such event where the proper conduction of events is not adhered to is termed as events abuse.

In many matches, public

mismanagements and misconducts are witnessed. Public throng events avenues and play havoc in it. They have been witnessed abusing participants. Such kind of public atrocities are common event abuse witnessed in almost all events.

Certain events have been found lacking adequate funds. These kinds of events can be witnessed in rallies and political gatherings where politicians depend upon others for money.

It has been a matter of utter shame and disgust when certain political speech arenas have been shared by political leaders and rich citizens alike. It is as if Political leaders are a puppet of such rich citizens. Such a shameful event was witnessed in Britain when Indian Prime Minister Shri Rajiv Gandhi and a Sikh Swaraj Paul shared the same platform delivering their speech views. It really is the example of event abuse and must be avoided. Prime Minister of a Nation is above citizens and citizen can express their views separately.

Events have been inappropriately conducted in the sense that its organizers could not spread their messages properly to masses. Such examples are also witnessed in today's world. Public or viewers have been found rising in revolt when the organizers were delivering their messages.

In certain events anti-National slogans have been heard thus arousing ghastly view regarding the event organizers and such Nations. Peoples have been found burning effigies of prominent leaders in the avenues of events. Such kind of malpractices gives the pathetic and sadist mentality of the peoples of such nations and it gives wrong attitudes about such nationals to World.

Horse trading, event criminalization and events politicization add to the events abuse list. Such practices mar the spirit of events and its organizers zeal.

It is a matter of great disgust to read such events abuse. Events are held to lubricate the lives of peoples. Proper awareness should be brought in the minds of peoples regarding events. Events must be learnt to be enjoyed and not abused. Whatever be the National and International scenario, events brotherhood and universal peace message must be adhered to.

Proper educated youth would not indulge in events abuse. During schools and colleges, proper ethics must be given to students so that they learn recreations of events in its proper sense.

World is fast developing and so are events. Events must not be abused, instead must be enjoyed thoroughly in its proper sense.

ABOUT THE AUTHOR

After my Commerce Degree, I ventured in various Multi-nationals at good Designations. I often wondered about authoring some good works. Finally, it started taking shape. I started writing small Articles and then it became bigger and bigger till finally becoming an Author. I with inspirations of my wife Mrs. Chandraprabha wish to serve Humanity through my Books and Writing which is really happening.